BEAUTY
RICO

Your Ultimate Travel Guide

By

Luis Diago

TABLE OF CONTENTS

INTRODUCTION 6

   Welcome to Puerto Rico 6

   Why Puerto Rico Should Be Your Next Destination 10

CHAPTER 1 EXPLORING PUERTO RICO'S HISTORY AND CULTURE 14

   A Brief Overview of Puerto Rico's History 14

   The Rich Cultural Heritage of Puerto Rico 18

   Must-Visit Museums and Historical Sites 22

CHAPTER 2 NATURAL WONDERS OF PUERTO RICO 26

   Discovering Puerto Rico's Diverse Ecosystems 26

   Exploring the El Yunque Rainforest 30

   Sun, Sand, and Surf: Puerto Rico's Beaches 33

   Caving Adventures in Rio Camuy Cave Park ... 37

CHAPTER 3 CUISINE AND CULINARY DELIGHTS 40

   Puerto Rican Cuisine: A Gastronomic Journey. 40

Dining Experiences and Food Markets............. 44

CHAPTER 4 VIBRANT CITIES AND CHARMING TOWNS... 48

Exploring San Juan: The Capital City 48

Ponce: The Pearl of the South........................... 52

Old San Juan: A Historic Gem.......................... 56

Visiting Quaint Towns and Villages.................. 60

CHAPTER 5 OUTDOOR ACTIVITIES AND ADVENTURES... 63

Hiking and Outdoor Adventures 63

Water Sports and Recreation............................. 67

Horseback Riding and Eco-Tours 70

CHAPTER 6 FESTIVALS AND CELEBRATIONS 73

A Calendar of Puerto Rico's Colorful Festivals 73

Joining in the Celebrations: Tips for Tourists ... 78

CHAPTER 7 PRACTICAL TRAVEL INFORMATION 81

Transportation and Getting Around 81

Accommodation Options: From Luxury Resorts to Cozy Inns 85

Packing Tips and Essentials 89

Traveling Responsibly in Puerto Rico 93

CHAPTER 8 PLANNING YOUR TRIP 97

Creating Your Puerto Rico Itinerary 97

Budgeting for Your Puerto Rico Vacation 102

Safety Tips for Travelers 105

CONCLUSION 108

Useful Phrases in Spanish 111

INTRODUCTION

Welcome to Puerto Rico

Puerto Rico, commonly referred to as the "Island of Enchantment," is a mesmerizing destination that lures tourists with its unique combination of natural beauty, rich history, lively culture, and friendly hospitality. Located in the northeastern Caribbean, this U.S. territory is a tropical paradise noted for its magnificent beaches, lush jungles, and various terrain. As you begin on your trip to experience the beauty of Puerto Rico, allow us to offer a warm welcome and introduce you to the magical world that awaits.

A Tropical Paradise: The instant you step foot on Puerto Rican land, you'll be met by the soft rustle of palm palms, the perfume of exotic flowers, and the calming sound of waves lapping against the beach. The island's tropical atmosphere, with typical temperatures ranging from the mid-70s to the mid-80s Fahrenheit year-round, providing the ideal background for outdoor excursions and leisure equally.

A Tapestry of Cultures: Puerto Rico is a melting pot of cultures, displaying the impact of indigenous Taíno, Spanish, African, and American traditions. This cultural tapestry is woven into every facet of Puerto Rican culture, from its food to its music and dance. Prepare to be charmed by the energetic rhythms of salsa, the colorful craftsmanship of local craftsmen, and the friendly smiles of the island's population, who are delighted to share their history with tourists.

Historical Significance: The history of Puerto Rico is a narrative of perseverance and reinvention. From its days as a Spanish colony to its position as a U.S. territory, Puerto Rico's history is apparent in its architecture, museums, and historic places. Explore centuries-old forts, meander through lovely colonial villages, and acquire a greater grasp of the island's history as you dig into its historical sites.

Natural Wonders: Nature aficionados will discover Puerto Rico to be a paradise of biodiversity. The El Yunque Rainforest, the only tropical rainforest in the U.S. National Forest System, has lush foliage, flowing waterfalls, and rich fauna. Meanwhile, magnificent beaches, bioluminescent bays, and stunning mountainscapes give infinite chances for outdoor exploration and adventure.

Your Ultimate Travel Guide: In this travel guide, we want to be your trusted companion while you traverse the delights of Puerto Rico. Whether you're a history enthusiast, a nature lover, a gourmet, or just seeking leisure under the Caribbean sun, Puerto Rico has something to offer every tourist. From practical travel recommendations to in-depth insights into the island's culture and attractions, this book will help you make the most of your stay.

So, dear traveler, as you open the pages of this book and begin your adventure through the magical world of Puerto Rico, let its beauty and charm capture your heart. The warm friendliness of its people, the depth of its culture, and the grandeur of its natural surroundings welcome you at every step. Welcome to Puerto Rico, where incredible memories and experiences are waiting to be found.

Why Puerto Rico Should Be Your Next Destination

When it comes to picking your next trip location, the globe is full with interesting destinations to discover. However, Puerto Rico stands out as a must-visit location for a plethora of reasons. Whether you're a nature enthusiast, a history buff, a gourmet lover, or just seeking a tropical paradise, Puerto Rico provides something for everyone. Here are five strong reasons why Puerto Rico should be at the top of your trip list:

Natural Beauty Beyond Compare: Puerto Rico is endowed with an incredible array of natural treasures. The island features gorgeous white-sand beaches that extend as far as the eye can see. Whether you're searching for a hidden cove or a bustling beach with water activities, Puerto Rico offers it all. The turquoise seas are great for swimming, snorkeling, surfing, and diving, making it a delight for water enthusiasts.

Inland, you'll encounter the verdant El Yunque Rainforest, a genuine natural wonder.

This tropical rainforest is home to unique flora and animals, hiking routes leading to gushing waterfalls, and panoramic landscapes that will take your breath away. Explore the magical Rio Camuy Cave Park, with its subterranean rivers and limestone formations, or trek into the rough Cordillera Central highlands for hiking and birding.

Rich Cultural Heritage: Puerto Rico's culture is a rich tapestry woven with threads from indigenous Taíno, Spanish, African, and American influences. You may experience this cultural richness in everything from the island's music and dancing to its art and food. Salsa music and dance are strongly embedded in Puerto Rican culture, and you'll find chances to immerse yourself in this bustling environment at clubs and festivals.

Don't miss the opportunity to experience the island's wonderful food, which mixes classic flavors with contemporary ingenuity. From mofongo (a mashed plantain dish) to arroz con gandules (rice with pigeon peas) and coquito (a coconut-based holiday drink),

Puerto Rico's food scene is a gastronomic journey waiting to be discovered.

Fascinating History and Architecture: As you travel Puerto Rico, you'll meet a rich tapestry of history. The island's history includes its period as a Spanish colony, which is visible in the colonial architecture of Old San Juan, where centuries-old forts like El Morro and San Cristóbal remain as testaments to the past. Wander through the cobblestone lanes of this ancient area, where colorful houses and plazas beg you to travel back in time.

Vibrant Cities and Charming Towns: Puerto Rico provides a combination of lively cities and picturesque communities to explore. San Juan, the capital city, is a lively centre of culture, entertainment, and shopping, while Ponce, known as the "Pearl of the South," oozes a relaxing appeal with its ancient architecture and cultural attractions. Beyond the cities, you'll discover scenic communities like Rincón, noted for its surfing, and Vieques, home to some of the world's brightest bioluminescent bays.

Accessibility and Convenience: Puerto Rico provides the ease of being a U.S. territory, which means no passport is necessary for U.S. citizens, and the currency is the U.S. dollar. English is commonly spoken, making it simple to converse, but Spanish lends a bit of authenticity to your visit.

Additionally, Puerto Rico is well-connected with direct flights from major U.S. cities, making it readily accessible for vacationers.

In conclusion, Puerto Rico's unique combination of natural beauty, cultural diversity, historical importance, and accessibility make it a great destination for a broad spectrum of people. Whether you want adventure in the great outdoors, cultural immersion, or just relaxation on the beach, Puerto Rico is ready to welcome you with open arms and a world of unique experiences. Make Puerto Rico your next vacation and let the charm of the island grab your heart.

CHAPTER 1 EXPLORING PUERTO RICO'S HISTORY AND CULTURE

A Brief Overview of Puerto Rico's History

The history of Puerto Rico is a rich and complicated fabric that spans thousands of years. From its indigenous beginnings through its colonial past and contemporary position as a U.S. territory, the island's history is a reflection of the numerous cultures and forces that have formed it. Here's a basic review of Puerto Rico's history:

Indigenous Inhabitants: Pre-Columbian Era: Long before the advent of European explorers, Puerto Rico was inhabited by the Taíno people. These original occupants had a complex society with a well-developed agricultural system, art, and religious rituals. They dubbed the island "Borikén," which inspired the contemporary name, Puerto Rico, meaning "rich port."

Spanish Colonization: 1493-1898: In 1493, Christopher Columbus landed in Puerto Rico on his second trip to the Americas. The Spanish colonization of the island started, and it became a vital transit site for Spanish ships going between Europe and the Americas. Over the years, Puerto Rico was significantly impacted by Spanish culture, and its economy depended on sugar cane, coffee, and other agricultural goods.

During this era, Puerto Rico also experienced obstacles, including invasions by opposing European countries and fights for autonomy. However, it remained a Spanish colony until 1898.

U.S. Rule: 1898-Present: In 1898, after the Spanish-American War, Puerto Rico was surrendered to the United States by the Treaty of Paris. The island became an unincorporated territory of the United States, marking the beginning of a new period in its history. Puerto Ricans were awarded U.S. citizenship in 1917, and the island's economy started to move towards manufacturing and industry.

Throughout the 20th century, Puerto Rico saw substantial economic development and modernization, but also faced problems such as political disagreements about its status. Puerto Ricans have conducted multiple referendums to decide their political destiny, with possibilities ranging from statehood to independence, but the subject remains unsolved.

Modern Puerto Rico: Today, Puerto Rico has a unique combination of cultures, with a mix of Spanish, African, Taíno, and American influences. Its culture is honored via music, dancing, art, and food. Salsa music, in particular, has become linked with Puerto Rican culture and is worldwide famous.

The island is noted for its outstanding natural beauty, including lush jungles, lovely beaches, and unusual bioluminescent bays. Tourism plays a vital part in the Puerto Rican economy, bringing people from across the globe.

Puerto Rico's political position is a matter of controversy and discussion, as some Puerto Ricans continue to campaign for statehood or independence, while others accept the status quo as a U.S. territory.

In conclusion, Puerto Rico's history is a tribute to its tenacity and flexibility in the face of shifting conditions and pressures. From its indigenous origins through its colonial past and present identity, Puerto Rico's history is a complicated and intriguing journey that has contributed to the island's distinctive cultural richness and variety. Understanding this past is crucial to appreciate the beauty and complexity of Puerto Rico today.

The Rich Cultural Heritage of Puerto Rico

Puerto Rico's cultural legacy is a complex tapestry woven from a varied variety of influences, including Indigenous, Spanish, African, and American traditions. This unusual combination has given life to a rich and vibrant culture that is both firmly anchored in history and continually growing. Here, we study the numerous components of Puerto Rico's cultural heritage:

Indigenous Roots: Taíno Heritage: Before the advent of Christopher Columbus in 1493, the Taíno people occupied Puerto Rico. Their heritage is still present in the island's language, food, and culture. Taíno influences may be observed in the names of numerous cities and sites in Puerto Rico, as well as in the island's native crops, such as cassava and sweet potatoes. Additionally, indigenous Taíno music and dance have left an unmistakable influence on Puerto Rican culture.

Spanish Influence: Colonial Heritage: Over the span of over 400 years of Spanish colonialism, Puerto Rico received a multitude of cultural aspects from its European invaders. Spanish architecture fills the alleys of Old San Juan, where centuries-old forts and colorful buildings take tourists back in time. The Spanish language remains the prevalent tongue, with a particular Puerto Rican accent and lexicon. The Roman Catholic religion, established by the Spanish, plays a prominent part in the island's culture, with various religious festivals and customs observed throughout the year.

African Rhythms: Musical and Dance Traditions: The African influence in Puerto Rico is especially noticeable in its music and dance. African rhythms, instruments, and dance techniques have been combined with Indigenous and European components to produce distinct Puerto Rican cultural traditions. Bomba, a classic Afro-Puerto Rican music and dancing form, highlights the rich African roots. The use of drums, call-and-response singing, and vivid costumes make it a dynamic and integral aspect of Puerto Rican culture.

Culinary Delights: Fusion of Flavors: Puerto Rican food is a lovely representation of the island's eclectic background. Staples including rice, beans, plantains, and yucca are consumed in many ways. Traditional foods like mofongo (mashed plantains with garlic and pork) and arroz con gandules (rice with pigeon peas) are appreciated by residents and tourists alike.

Festivals and Celebrations: Puerto Rico is noted for its vivid festivals and festivities, which give a glimpse into its culture and history. These ceremonies generally integrate Indigenous, Spanish, and African customs. The San Sebastián Street Festival in San Juan and the Vejigantes Festival in Ponce are only two examples of exuberant, colorful festivals that incorporate music, dancing, parades, and extravagant masks and costumes.

Arts & Crafts: Puerto Rico has a strong arts scene, with a diverse spectrum of artistic and performing arts. Local craftsmen manufacture elaborate products, including traditional vejigante masks, santos (saint statues), and bright linens. Puerto Rican painters, sculptors, and musicians have made major contributions to both the national and worldwide art sectors.

Language and Literature: Puerto Rican literature, both in Spanish and English, has produced great writers and poets such Julia de Burgos, Pedro Juan Soto, and Esmeralda Santiago. The island's linguistic environment reflects its eclectic background, with a unique Puerto Rican Spanish dialect influenced by Indigenous, African, and European languages.

In conclusion, Puerto Rico's rich cultural legacy is a monument to its historical variety and persistence. Its people take pleasure in conserving their traditions while accepting innovation and progress. Whether you're exploring the music, dancing, cuisine, or festivals, immersing yourself in Puerto Rico's cultural legacy gives a better knowledge of the island's essence and a more enjoyable travel experience.

Must-Visit Museums and Historical Sites

Puerto Rico is a treasure mine of history and culture, with a vast choice of museums and historical sites that give intriguing insights into the island's past and present. Whether you're a history buff, an art lover, or just anxious to discover the legacy of this Caribbean treasure, here are five must-visit museums and historical places in Puerto Rico:

Old San Juan: The whole historic area of Old San Juan is a living museum in itself. The picturesque cobblestone alleys, colorful colonial homes, and majestic forts, such as El Morro and San Cristóbal, are UNESCO World Heritage Sites. Explore the San Juan National Historic Site to learn about the city's position as a Spanish colonial bastion and its strategic importance in securing the Caribbean.

Museo de Arte de Puerto Rico (MAPR): Located in San Juan, MAPR is the island's principal art museum. It has a remarkable collection of Puerto Rican art extending from the 17th century to modern works. The museum shows a broad variety of creative genres and materials, including paintings, sculptures, and decorative arts.

Museo de las Américas: Situated in the ancient Cuartel de Ballajá in Old San Juan, the Museo de las Américas dives into the history, culture, and art of the Americas, with a special concentration on Puerto Rico. The exhibitions examine the island's indigenous past, Spanish colonial era, African influences, and more.

Caguana Indigenous Ceremonial Park: Located in Utuado, Caguana Indigenous Ceremonial Park is a crucial trip for people interested in the Taíno culture. The park has recreated Taíno ceremonial ball courts and petroglyphs, offering insight into the island's pre-Columbian past.

Ponce Museum of Art: This museum in Ponce features a comprehensive collection of European, Latin American, and Puerto Rican art. Its European collection contains works by notable painters including Velázquez, Goya, and Rubens. The museum's excellent collection of Puerto Rican art encompasses numerous eras and genres.

Casa Blanca: Casa Blanca is a historic home museum in Old San Juan that was previously the residence of the Ponce de León family. Visitors may visit the wonderfully restored buildings, gardens, and displays that give an insight into the lifestyle of the island's colonial aristocracy.

Cemí Museum: Located in Jayuya, the Cemí Museum honors the Taíno culture and shows a significant collection of Taíno antiquities, including ceramics, stone sculptures, and ceremonial items. It's a rare chance to learn about the indigenous history of Puerto Rico.

El Cid Historic Cultural Center: Situated in the charming village of Rincón, the El Cid Historic Cultural Center is set in a magnificently renovated 18th-century structure. The center provides exhibitions and events that showcase the history and culture of the area, with a special emphasis on the significance of art and artists.

San Germán Historic District: San Germán, one of Puerto Rico's oldest municipalities, features a historic neighborhood with well-preserved colonial buildings. Stroll through its streets to uncover magnificent churches, plazas, and museums, such as the Porta Coeli Church Museum, which is one of the oldest churches in the Americas.

Tibes Indigenous Ceremonial Center: Located in Ponce, the Tibes Indigenous Ceremonial Center gives a unique chance to experience the history and culture of the Taíno people. The site comprises archaeological digs, rebuilt Taíno buildings, and exhibitions that provide insight on the island's indigenous history.

These museums and historical places give a thrilling trip through the layers of Puerto Rico's history, culture, and art. Whether you're interested in ancient civilizations, colonial history, or contemporary art, Puerto Rico provides a multitude of activities that will improve your appreciation for this lovely island.

CHAPTER 2 NATURAL WONDERS OF PUERTO RICO

Discovering Puerto Rico's Diverse Ecosystems

Puerto Rico, popularly referred to as the "Island of Enchantment," is not only rich in history and culture but also features a breathtaking variety of varied ecosystems. From lush jungles to beautiful beaches, caverns, mountains, and unique bioluminescent bays, Puerto Rico provides nature aficionados and outdoor explorers a multitude of possibilities to explore and enjoy its natural splendor. Here's a deeper look at some of the island's amazing ecosystems:

El Yunque Rainforest: El Yunque National Forest, frequently simply called El Yunque, is the only tropical rainforest in the U.S. National Forest System. Located in the northeast of Puerto Rico, El Yunque is a lush paradise with thick vegetation, gushing waterfalls, and a network of well-maintained hiking routes. As you explore further into the jungle, you'll meet unusual flora and animals, like the coquí frog, several varieties of orchids, and colorful birds. The El Yunque experience is a must for anybody seeking immersion in a tropical jungle.

Pristine Beaches: Puerto Rico is recognized for its stunning beaches, each giving its own particular appeal. Whether you like the quiet sands of Flamenco Beach on Culebra Island, the exuberant surf of Rincon Beach on the west coast, or the crystal-clear seas of Luquillo Beach on the east coast, you'll find a beach to fit your tastes. Snorkeling, swimming, surfing, or just lazing on the sandy shoreline, Puerto Rico's beaches are great for leisure and water-based activity.

Caving Adventures: For spelunking aficionados and those interested about subterranean marvels, Puerto Rico offers various unique cave systems to explore. The Rio Camuy Cave Park has one of the world's biggest cave networks, featuring subterranean rivers, immense chambers, and stunning limestone structures. The Cueva Ventana, or "Window Cave," provides stunning views of the verdant environment from inside a natural cave entrance.

Coastal Mangroves and Estuaries: The island's coastline portions are lined with mangrove forests and estuaries, which serve as essential homes for several types of fauna and birds. Take a kayak or boat excursion through these mangroves, like those in the Fajardo Bio Bay, and observe the natural beauty that lives in these distinct ecosystems. Some of the bays even display bioluminescence, producing a magnificent light show as you paddle around the waters at night.

Cordillera Central Mountains: Puerto Rico's interior is dominated by the Cordillera Central mountain range. Adventure seekers may climb the beautiful routes, such as those in Guanica State Forest or Maricao State Forest, to explore the island's rocky interior. These mountains provide spectacular landscapes, waterfalls, and a chance to watch local creatures in their natural setting.

Dry Forests and Unique Plant Life: The Guánica Dry Forest Reserve on the southwestern coast of the island is a UNESCO Biosphere Reserve and an unusual example of a subtropical dry forest ecosystem. This unusual ecosystem is home to several rare and endangered plant species, including the cactus-like Guayacán tree, which explodes into bright flower during the dry season.

Bioluminescent Bays: Puerto Rico is home to three of the world's most beautiful bioluminescent bays: Mosquito Bay in Vieques, Laguna Grande in Fajardo, and La Parguera in Lajas. These bays contain microorganisms that create a magnificent blue-green light when disturbed, producing a bizarre and mesmerizing nocturnal scene..

Exploring Puerto Rico's different ecosystems enables you to connect with the island's natural history and enjoy its tremendous variety. Whether you're trekking through a jungle, sunbathing on a beautiful beach, or kayaking through bioluminescent seas, each environment provides a distinct and amazing experience in this tropical paradise.

Exploring the El Yunque Rainforest

Nestled in the eastern portion of Puerto Rico, El Yunque National Forest is a lush and enchanting tropical rainforest, frequently referred to as the "Green Island" or the "Island of Enchantment." It's the only tropical rainforest inside the U.S. National Forest System and gives a fantastic chance for visitors to immerse themselves in nature's beauty and richness. Here's how to get the most of your tour in El Yunque Rainforest:

Getting There: El Yunque is situated approximately an hour's drive from San Juan, making it a popular day-trip destination. You may hire a vehicle, join a guided trip, or utilize public transit to reach the forest.

Visitor Center: Start your tour at the El Yunque Visitor Center, where you can collect information, pick up maps, and learn about the rainforest's vegetation, animals, and hiking paths. The center is a fantastic spot to orient oneself before exploring farther.

Hiking Trails: El Yunque provides a network of well-maintained hiking routes, each delivering a distinct rainforest experience. Some popular paths include:

La Mina trek: This trek leads to the spectacular La Mina Falls, where you may bathe in the soothing waters.

El Yunque Trail: Hike to the highest mountain in El Yunque for stunning panoramic views of the rainforest and beach.

Coca Falls walk: A short and simple walk going to the lovely Coca Falls.

Wildlife and Flora: Keep an eye out for the different fauna that makes El Yunque home. You could notice colorful parrots, tree frogs known as coquís, and other types of reptiles and insects. The rainforest is also home to a diversity of tropical vegetation, including huge ferns, orchids, and the gorgeous sierra palm.

Waterfalls and Swimming Holes: El Yunque is notable for its flowing waterfalls and natural ponds. Take a plunge in the clean, refreshing waters at sites like La Mina Falls and Juan Diego Falls. Remember to wear suitable swimwear and bring a towel.

Guided Tours: Consider taking a guided tour to improve your rainforest experience. Knowledgeable guides may give insights on the forest's ecology, history, and mythology.

Responsible Exploration: Practice responsible tourism by remaining on approved paths, disposing of waste appropriately, and preserving the natural environment. Leave no trace to protect the rainforest's preservation.

Exploring El Yunque Rainforest is a mesmerizing voyage into a world of lush foliage, refreshing waterfalls, and lively fauna. It's a natural sanctuary where you can reconnect with nature, enjoy the beauties of biodiversity, and experience the romance of a tropical rainforest right inside the United States.

Sun, Sand, and Surf: Puerto Rico's Beaches

Puerto Rico, with its rich surroundings and colorful culture, is arguably best known for its gorgeous beaches. With over 270 miles of coastline, this Caribbean island provides a diversity of beaches that suit to any traveler's interests, from peaceful coves to bustling surf locations. Here's a glance into the world of sun, sand, and surf that greets you on Puerto Rico's gorgeous shores:

Flamenco Beach, Culebra Island: Flamenco Beach frequently ranks among the world's greatest beaches, and with good reason. Located on the little island of Culebra, reachable by boat or small aircraft, Flamenco Beach is a paradise of pure white sand and crystal-clear seas. The horseshoe-shaped bay is great for swimming and snorkeling, with colorful fish and coral reefs near offshore. The beach's distinctive rusted tank, a legacy from the island's military past, provides a unique touch to the surroundings.

Luquillo Beach, Luquillo: Luquillo Beach, also referred to as "La Monserrate," is a family-friendly location on the northeast coast of Puerto Rico. This palm-fringed beach has mild waves, making it great for swimming and wading. The neighborhood is packed with food vendors dishing up wonderful local cuisine, enabling you to sample authentic Puerto Rican flavors while enjoying the coastal view.

Playa Rincon, Las Marias: Playa Rincon, on the west coast of the island, is recognized for its natural beauty and calm ambience. It's a little off the usual route, but the trek is definitely worth it. The beach is bordered by beautiful green hills and features golden beaches and quiet waves, making it a perfect site for relaxing and picnics.

Crash Boat Beach, Aguadilla: Crash Boat Beach is a popular among surfers and water sports enthusiasts. Its soft waves and steady swells give great conditions for surfing, kiteboarding, and windsurfing. The beach also offers a gorgeous pier where you may plunge into the clean waters or just enjoy the scenery.

Playa Flamenco, Culebra Island: While Culebra Island is home to numerous magnificent beaches, Playa Flamenco is another treasure not to be missed. It boasts gorgeous dunes, shallow blue seas, and an appealing ambience. The beach's tranquil waters make it great for snorkeling, while the neighboring hills give good climbing options.

Jobos Beach, Isabela: Jobos Beach is a notable surf location on the northwest coast of Puerto Rico. Surrounded by rugged cliffs and rich flora, the beach provides steady waves and a peaceful ambiance. Surf schools and rental shops are available for anyone wishing to catch some waves, while seaside bars offer an ideal area to unwind after a day of surfing.

Sun Bay Beach, Vieques Island: Vieques Island's Sun Bay Beach, commonly known as Playa La Playuela, is a serene and attractive area with shallow, calm waves. The beach is great for swimming, sunbathing, and picnics. The neighboring bioluminescent Mosquito Bay is another must-see site on Vieques.

Playa Sucia, Cabo Rojo: Playa Sucia, or "Dirty Beach," is everything but filthy. This secluded beach in Cabo Rojo is famed for its golden beaches, blue waves, and spectacular limestone cliffs. It's a lovely area for a calm vacation and is situated inside the Cabo Rojo National Wildlife Refuge.

Shacks Beach, Isabela: Shacks Beach is a known snorkeling site situated near Jobos Beach. Its quiet, clear waters and diverse marine life make it a paradise for underwater exploration. The beach also provides excellent views of Desecheo Island and is a fantastic area for beachcombing and resting.

Whether you're seeking excitement in the surf, a serene hideaway, or just a day of sunbathing and swimming, Puerto Rico's beaches have something to offer everyone. These gorgeous coastline attractions are not only attractive but also a tribute to the natural splendor and different landscapes that make Puerto Rico an outstanding tourism destination.

Caving Adventures in Rio Camuy Cave Park

Nestled in the midst of Puerto Rico's beautiful karst area, the Río Camuy Cave Park (Parque de las Cavernas del Río Camuy) provides an underground realm of wonder and awe that invites explorers and nature lovers alike. This remarkable geological gem is one of the biggest cave systems in the Western Hemisphere and delivers an unsurpassed caving experience. Here's a taste into the fascinating caving activities that await in Río Camuy Cave Park:

Discovering the Underground Realm: Río Camuy Cave Park is a wide network of limestone caverns and sinkholes created over millions of years by the Río Camuy, one of the world's third-largest underground rivers. The park offers more than 16 entrances to the caverns, with Cueva Clara being the most renowned and accessible.

Cueva Clara: Cueva Clara, or Clara Cave, serves as the major attraction inside the park. As you descend into the cave's depths, you'll be astounded by the sheer vastness and detailed beauty of its chambers. Massive stalactites hang from the ceilings, while stalagmites emerge from the cave floor, producing bizarre structures that look almost alien. The cave's huge chambers, such as the Cueva Clara and the Cueva Alfredo, provide numerous options for exploration and photography.

The Natural Cathedral: One of the features of Cueva Clara is the "Natural Cathedral," a huge hall with a towering roof that spans over 170 feet high. The cathedral-like acoustics provide a strange audio experience that visitors frequently describe as spiritual. The sounds of dripping water and the voices of other explorers intensify the feeling of awe in this subterranean refuge.

Cave Tours and Visitor Experience: Visitors to Río Camuy Cave Park may go on guided cave excursions lead by trained park rangers. These trips give insight into the geological processes that built the caverns, as well as the history and ecology of the region. There are many tour packages available, catering to varied degrees of curiosity and comfort.

Safety and Accessibility: It's crucial to realize that although the caverns are a spectacular sight, they may be tough to traverse. The terrain may be rough, slippery, and at times, challenging. Visitors should be in generally excellent physical condition and wear proper attire and footwear. Flashlights, helmets, and other equipment are normally given by the park.

Planning Your Visit: Río Camuy Cave Park is situated in the municipality of Lares in northern Puerto Rico. It's essential to verify the park's operating hours and tour availability in advance, since they might change seasonally and due to maintenance or weather conditions.

For caving aficionados and nature lovers, Río Camuy Cave Park provides a unique trip into the heart of Puerto Rico's underground universe. With its beautiful geological formations, vivid rainforest environs, and intriguing excursions, this natural marvel is a must-visit site for visitors wishing to uncover the hidden gems of the island.

CHAPTER 3 CUISINE AND CULINARY DELIGHTS

Puerto Rican Cuisine: A Gastronomic Journey

Puerto Rico's food is a colorful and savory expression of its rich cultural past and vast agricultural wealth. With influences from Spain, Africa, the Taíno indigenous people, and the United States, Puerto Rican cuisine is a delectable blend of tastes, textures, and traditions. Embark on a gastronomic trip as we explore the delectable and unusual world of Puerto Rican food.

Mofongo: A Puerto Rican Classic Mofongo is frequently regarded the archetypal Puerto Rican meal. It comprises of green plantains that are cooked and then mashed with garlic, olive oil, and occasionally chicharrones (crispy pig skin). The finished mixture is moulded into a ball or molded onto a plate and generally served with a delicious soup or sauce. Mofongo may be complemented with a number of toppings, including shrimp, chicken, or beef, making it a diverse and gratifying option.

Arroz with Gandules: A Flavorful Staple: Arroz with gandules, or rice with pigeon peas, is a mainstay of Puerto Rican cuisine and sometimes referred to as the island's "national dish." This fragrant rice dish mixes white rice with pigeon peas, green olives, capers, and a combination of spices, including sofrito (a mixture of aromatic herbs including peppers, onions, and garlic). It's a tasty and comforting meal commonly served at family gatherings and special events.

Lechón Asado: The King of Roasts: Lechón asado, or roast pig, is a favorite Puerto Rican dish. The entire pig is marinated with a fragrant combination of spices and herbs, then gently roasted on a spit or in an oven until the skin becomes crispy and the flesh soft and luscious. Lechón asado is generally the highlight of celebratory gatherings and festivities.

Tostones and Amarillos: Irresistible Plantain Delights: Plantains are a versatile element in Puerto Rican cuisine, and tostones and amarillos are two common methods to cook them. Tostones are green plantains that are cut, fried, crushed, and then cooked again to form crispy, flavorful chips. Amarillos, on the other hand, are ripe plantains that are sliced and fried to a sweet and caramelized perfection. These plantain recipes may be served as appetizers or sides.

Bacalao Guisado: A Flavorful Salted Cod Stew: Bacalao guisado is a delicious stew cooked with salted codfish, tomatoes, onions, and a mix of fragrant spices. The cod is first soaked to eliminate excess salt and then cooked with other seasonings to make a rich and substantial meal. It's a monument to Puerto Rico's connection to the sea and its ability to convert modest ingredients into a culinary marvel.

Coquito: The Iconic Puerto Rican Holiday Drink: Coquito is a creamy, coconut-based festive drink that is commonly referred to as "Puerto Rican eggnog." This delectable mixture is created with coconut cream, condensed milk, rum, and a dash of cinnamon and nutmeg. It's a must-have throughout the holiday season and is commonly shared with friends and family as a joyful custom.

Pasteles: A Labor of Love: Pasteles are a labor-intensive Puerto Rican meal that mimics tamales. They are created with grated green plantains and yautía (taro root), packed with a delicious combination of meat, olives, capers, and raisins, and then wrapped in banana leaves and cooked or steamed. Pasteles are generally a favorite holiday meal, cooked with care and eaten with loved ones.

Coffee: A Puerto Rican Pride: Puerto Rico is recognized for producing high-quality coffee, and a cup of Puerto Rican coffee is a must-try for caffeine addicts. The island's coffee is cultivated in the central hilly area and has a rich and powerful taste. Be sure to taste a cup of freshly made Puerto Rican coffee while traveling the island.

Puerto Rican food is a celebration of culture, history, and the island's natural richness. Whether you're tasting the tastes of a classic meal like mofongo or indulging in a sweet coquito, the culinary trip across Puerto Rico is a sensory experience that embodies the spirit of this wonderful Caribbean location.

Dining Experiences and Food Markets

When it comes to eating in Puerto Rico, you're in for a gastronomic journey that tantalizes your taste senses and immerses you in the lively culture of the island. From traditional family-owned restaurants to bustling food markets, Puerto Rico provides a broad assortment of eating experiences that appeal to every appetite. Here's a look into the world of eating and food markets in Puerto Rico:

Local Restaurants (Fondas and Lechoneras): Fondas are tiny, family-owned eateries that provide traditional Puerto Rican food with a home-cooked ambiance. These hidden jewels may be discovered around the island, sometimes in modest locales, and provide genuine tastes that embody the spirit of Puerto Rican food. Don't miss the opportunity to eat a lunch at a fonda for a sense of local life.

Lechoneras specialize in lechón asado, or roast pig, and are popular across Puerto Rico. These roadside eateries roast entire pigs on a spit, resulting in delicious, savory meat with crispy skin. The pleasure of eating lechón at a lechonera is a typical Puerto Rican gastronomic encounter.

Food Markets (Mercados de Comida): La Placita de Santurce is a busy food market in San Juan that comes alive in the evenings. Here, you'll discover a variety of food sellers and small cafes selling anything from traditional Puerto Rican delicacies to foreign cuisine. The environment is vibrant, with live music and dancing, making it a fantastic spot to appreciate local cuisine and culture.

Luquillo Kiosks: Located in Luquillo, on the east coast of Puerto Rico, the Luquillo Kiosks are a collection of open-air food booths and kiosks providing a broad range of meals. From seafood to classic Puerto Rican street cuisine like alcapurrias and bacalaitos, these booths are a food lover's heaven. It's a terrific venue to enjoy a range of local cuisines in a relaxing, beachfront atmosphere.

Mercado de Santurce: The Mercado de Santurce is a popular food market in San Juan's Santurce area. This contemporary market provides a varied choice of food sellers, craft items, and cafes. It's a terrific spot to enjoy creative Puerto Rican cuisine and find unusual culinary products and crafts.

Food Trucks and Street Food: Food trucks and street food sellers are a familiar sight across Puerto Rico. They provide easy and appetizing choices for meals on the move. Look out for famous street dishes like empanadillas (fried turnovers stuffed with different ingredients), alcapurrias, and pinchos (skewers of marinated pork).

Traditional Bakery Cafés (Panaderías and Cafetines) Local panaderías (bakeries) and cafetines (little cafes) are perfect locations to sample Puerto Rican sweets and coffee. Enjoy staples like pastelillos (stuffed pastries), quesitos (cream cheese-filled pastries), and freshly brewed Puerto Rican coffee in a pleasant and welcoming ambiance.

Gastronomic Tours: For a guided culinary experience, try joining a gastronomy tour in San Juan or other major cities. These trips generally include visits to local restaurants, food markets, and street food sellers, enabling you to try a broad selection of Puerto Rican foods while learning about the island's culinary legacy.

Fine Dining and Fusion Cuisine: Puerto Rico also boasts a sophisticated dining scene with restaurants that mix native Puerto Rican cuisine with foreign influences. These places generally showcase imaginative and innovative meals that raise the island's food to new heights.

Exploring dining experiences and food markets in Puerto Rico is not just about eating; it's a voyage into the heart of the island's culture and history. Whether you're relishing traditional foods in a fonda, experiencing street food at a kiosk, or indulging in gourmet cuisine, each dining experience delivers a distinct sense of Puerto Rico's rich culinary history.

CHAPTER 4 VIBRANT CITIES AND CHARMING TOWNS

Exploring San Juan: The Capital City

San Juan, the capital city of Puerto Rico, is a dynamic and intriguing destination that perfectly integrates history, culture, and modernity. Nestled on the northeastern coast of the island, San Juan is not only the cultural and economic core of Puerto Rico but also a UNESCO World Heritage Site with a rich tapestry of experiences awaiting tourists. Here's a stroll around the gorgeous streets and sites of San Juan:

Old San Juan: A Historic Gem: Begin your trip in Old San Juan, a historic region famed for its colorful colonial buildings and cobblestone pathways. The neighborhood is encompassed by huge defenses, including El Morro and San Cristóbal forts, which played a significant role in safeguarding the city against pirates and invaders. Explore the walls, climb the sentry towers, and take in the beautiful views of the Atlantic Ocean.

As you travel around Old San Juan, you'll see vivid facades, pleasant plazas, and attractive eateries. Be sure to visit La Fortaleza, the oldest executive home in continuous use in the Americas, and El Convento, a former convent turned luxury hotel with a magnificent courtyard.

Calle San Sebastián Festival: A Celebration of Culture: If your visit coincides with the annual Calle San Sebastián Festival, you're in for a treat. Held in January, this bustling street festival combines live music, dancing performances, art exhibits, and delectable street cuisine, creating a lively and celebratory environment that portrays Puerto Rican culture at its finest.

Cuisine and Dining: A Gastronomic Adventure: San Juan is a gastronomic heaven with an abundance of eating alternatives. Explore neighborhood eateries, or fondas, to sample classic Puerto Rican meals like mofongo, arroz con gandules, and lechón asado.

Don't forget to enjoy the varied fusion food offered in the city's premium restaurants, where traditional flavors meet contemporary culinary methods.

La Placita de Santurce: In the evenings, travel to this vibrant market in the Santurce district for a genuine Puerto Rican eating experience. Sample a range of local delicacies, enjoy live music, and immerse yourself in the joyful environment.

El Yunque National Forest: Nature's Oasis: Just a short drive from San Juan, you may explore the El Yunque National Forest, the only tropical rainforest in the U.S. National Forest System. Hike its picturesque pathways, bathe in freshwater pools under tumbling waterfalls, and listen to the enchanting sounds of the rainforest's fauna.

Condado and Isla Verde Beaches: Coastal Bliss: For sun, sea, and relaxation, come to the lovely Condado and Isla Verde beaches. These urban beaches provide a wonderful combination of natural beauty and city comforts, with lots of waterfront resorts, bars, and restaurants. Enjoy swimming, water sports, or just sunbathing in the Caribbean heat.

Viejo San Juan Nightlife: Dancing and Entertainment: As night falls, Viejo San Juan comes alive with a thriving nightlife scene. Explore the bustling pubs, clubs, and music venues that provide everything from salsa dancing to live jazz concerts.

San Juan's Museums and Art Galleries: For art and culture aficionados, San Juan features a range of museums and galleries. Explore the Museo de Arte de Puerto Rico for a complete collection of Puerto Rican art, visit the Museum of Contemporary Art, or immerse yourself in the island's history in the Museo de las Américas in Old San Juan.

San Juan's combination of history, culture, and natural beauty makes it an appealing destination for tourists seeking a unique and rewarding experience. Whether you're exploring centuries-old forts, dancing to salsa rhythms, or sampling local cuisine, San Juan welcomes you to immerse yourself in the spirit of Puerto Rico.

Ponce: The Pearl of the South

Ponce, sometimes referred to as "The Pearl of the South" (La Perla del Sur), is a gorgeous and culturally rich city situated on the southern coast of Puerto Rico. With its combination of historic charm, bustling art scene, and magnificent natural beauty, Ponce is a must-visit destination that gives guests a unique and original Puerto Rican experience. Here's a stroll around the wonderful city of Ponce:

Plaza Las Delicias: The Heart of Ponce: Start your journey of Ponce in Plaza Las Delicias, the city's major center and gathering area. This busy plaza is surrounded by prominent structures, including the Cathedral of Our Lady of Guadalupe and the Luis A. Ferré Performing Arts Center, recognized for its unique white exterior and colorful cultural acts. The square is also home to the Parque de Bombas, a historic firehouse-turned-museum that has become a symbol of Ponce.

Museo de Arte de Ponce: A World-Class Collection: The Museo de Arte de Ponce is one of Puerto Rico's major art museums, with a significant collection of European, American, and Puerto Rican art. The museum's exquisite neoclassical edifice holds works by famous painters like as Velázquez, Rubens, and Goya, as well as a substantial collection of Puerto Rican art spanning several ages.

Historic District and Architecture: Ponce's historic area is a treasure trove of spectacular architecture and wonderfully restored structures. Stroll along the cobblestone alleys and observe the colonial-style residences embellished with colorful facades, elaborate balconies, and lush tropical gardens. The city's dedication to maintaining its architectural legacy is obvious in its well-maintained historic areas.

Hacienda Buena Vista: Coffee and Conservation: Explore the Hacienda Buena Vista, a restored 19th-century coffee plantation that provides guided tours. Learn about Puerto Rico's coffee history and the plantation's importance in the island's agricultural past. The hacienda also promotes the significance of environmental protection and sustainable agricultural techniques.

La Guancha Boardwalk: Waterfront Relaxation: For a peaceful day by the ocean, come to La Guancha Boardwalk. This busy waterfront neighborhood provides coastal eating, souvenir stores, and a lovely environment. It's a fantastic site to savor fresh seafood, watch the sunset, or take a leisurely stroll down the boardwalk.

Carnaval de Ponce: A Festive Tradition: If your vacation coincides with February or early March, don't miss the Carnaval de Ponce, one of Puerto Rico's most recognized and vibrant festivities. The city comes alive with parades, live music, dancing, and spectacular costumes, making it a bright and celebratory event.

Ponce, "The Pearl of the South," is a city that encompasses the spirit of Puerto Rico's rich history and lively culture. From its lovely plazas and ancient architecture to its world-class art museum and bustling festivals, Ponce welcomes tourists to experience the cultural richness and natural beauties that make it a remarkable destination in the Caribbean.

Old San Juan: A Historic Gem

Old San Juan, or "Viejo San Juan" in Spanish, is a historic district that stands as a testament to Puerto Rico's rich cultural heritage and colonial past. This enchanting walled city, perched on the northwestern coast of Puerto Rico, is a UNESCO World Heritage Site and one of the most iconic and picturesque destinations in the Caribbean. Let's embark on a journey through the captivating streets and landmarks of Old San Juan:

Cobblestone Streets and Colorful Facades: Old San Juan's narrow, cobblestone streets are a photographer's dream, lined with vibrantly colored buildings that range from pastel hues to bright shades of blue, pink, and yellow. As you wander through the historic district, you'll be immersed in a visually stunning and Instagram-worthy environment.

El Morro and San Cristóbal Forts: Dominating the coastline of Old San Juan are two imposing fortresses: El Morro (Castillo San Felipe del Morro) and San Cristóbal (Castillo San Cristóbal). These historic forts, built by the Spanish to protect the city from pirates and invaders, offer a glimpse into Puerto Rico's military history. Explore the tunnels, ramparts, and sentry towers while enjoying panoramic views of the Atlantic Ocean.

La Fortaleza: Governor's Mansion: La Fortaleza, also known as the Palacio de Santa Catalina, is the oldest executive mansion in continuous use in the Americas. This elegant colonial structure serves as the official residence of the Governor of Puerto Rico. While you can't tour the interior, you can admire its stunning facade and architecture from the outside.

Parque de las Palomas: Pigeon Park: Parque de las Palomas, or Pigeon Park, is a charming open square where hundreds of pigeons congregate. It's a peaceful spot where you can relax, feed the pigeons, and enjoy the tranquility of Old San Juan amidst the hustle and bustle of the city.

Calle del Cristo: Shopping and Souvenirs: Calle del Cristo, one of the main streets in Old San Juan, is lined with boutique shops and galleries selling unique Puerto Rican crafts, artwork, and jewelry. It's a perfect place to find souvenirs and gifts that capture the essence of the island's culture.

Casa Blanca: Historic Residence: Casa Blanca is a historic house in Old San Juan, once the residence of Juan Ponce de León, the first Governor of Puerto Rico. Today, it is a museum that offers insights into the island's history and the life of its early European

As evening falls, Old San Juan transforms into a lively nightlife hub. Explore the vibrant bars, clubs, and music venues for a dose of salsa dancing, live jazz, or simply to enjoy a cocktail with a view of the illuminated city.

Old San Juan is a living testament to Puerto Rico's rich history, vibrant culture, and architectural beauty. Whether you're strolling through its historic streets, exploring centuries-old forts, or savoring local cuisine, this historic gem offers a captivating glimpse into the island's past and a memorable experience for all who visit.

Visiting Quaint Towns and Villages

While Puerto Rico is known for its bustling cities and beautiful beaches, the island also boasts a collection of charming towns and villages that offer a more relaxed and authentic Caribbean experience. These quaint locales, often nestled in the mountains or along the coast, provide a glimpse into Puerto Rico's rich cultural heritage and natural beauty. Here are some of the must-visit towns and villages that showcase the island's unique charm:

Rincón: The Surfing Capital: Located on the west coast of Puerto Rico, Rincón is a laid-back beach town known for its world-class surfing and stunning sunsets. The town's relaxed atmosphere and beautiful beaches make it a favorite among surfers, beach lovers, and nature enthusiasts. Don't miss the opportunity to watch the surfers ride the waves at popular spots like Sandy Beach.

Culebra: A Caribbean Paradise: The island municipality of Culebra, just east of Puerto Rico, is a tropical paradise known for its pristine beaches and crystal-clear waters. Flamenco Beach, often cited as one of the world's best beaches, is a must-visit destination on the island. Culebra's relaxed vibe, snorkeling opportunities, and vibrant marine life make it a perfect escape from the mainland.

Vieques: A Bioluminescent Wonder: Located just off the east coast of Puerto Rico, Vieques is another enchanting island municipality. It's renowned for the stunning Mosquito Bay, one of the world's brightest bioluminescent bays. Visitors can kayak or take guided night tours to witness the magical glow of the water caused by tiny, glowing microorganisms.

Aibonito: The Garden of Puerto Rico: Known as "La Ciudad de las Flores" (The City of Flowers), Aibonito is a mountain town nestled in the Central Range of Puerto Rico. Its cool climate and fertile soil make it a haven for horticulture and floriculture. Visit the Aibonito Flower Festival in early January to witness an explosion of colors and fragrances.

Lares: A Cultural Gem: Lares is a town rich in history and culture, known for the Grito de Lares, a significant event in Puerto Rican history that took place in 1868. The town's central plaza, historic churches, and traditional architecture provide a glimpse into Puerto Rico's past.

Isabela: Beaches and Surfing: Isabela, on the northwest coast, is a haven for surfers and beach lovers. With its charming small-town vibe, gorgeous beaches like Jobos Beach, and a vibrant surfing culture, Isabela is a hidden gem for those seeking a quieter coastal experience.

Exploring these quaint towns and villages in Puerto Rico allows travelers to step off the beaten path and discover the island's hidden treasures. Whether you're looking for natural beauty, cultural immersion, or a taste of traditional Caribbean life, these charming locales offer a diverse range of experiences that showcase the unique character of Puerto Rico.

CHAPTER 5 OUTDOOR ACTIVITIES AND ADVENTURES

Hiking and Outdoor Adventures

Puerto Rico is a tropical paradise that provides much more than simply lovely beaches. The island's numerous landscapes, from lush rainforests to craggy mountains, offer the ideal setting for outdoor enthusiasts and nature lovers. Whether you're an expert hiker or a casual explorer, Puerto Rico's hiking and outdoor experiences provide a multitude of possibilities to connect with nature and enjoy the island's natural treasures. Here's a taste of the outdoor experiences that await you:

El Yunque National Forest: Tropical Rainforest Hiking: El Yunque National Forest is the only tropical rainforest in the United States National Forest System and a must-visit for nature aficionados. It provides a network of well-maintained hiking routes that range in intensity, from short hikes to strenuous expeditions. The paths carry you through lush forest, through waterfalls, and up to magnificent vistas. Don't miss the opportunity to climb to La Mina Falls, one of the most spectacular waterfalls in the jungle.

Toro Negro Forest: Mountains and Waterfalls: Located in the middle highlands of Puerto Rico, the Toro Negro Forest is another trekking heaven. The park's pathways lead you through lush wooded regions, through dazzling waterfalls, and up to the peak of Cerro de Punta, the highest point in Puerto Rico. The expedition gives amazing views of the surrounding mountains and valleys.

Guánica Dry Forest Reserve: Unique Ecosystems: The Guánica Dry Forest Reserve, a UNESCO World Heritage Site, is a rare dry forest environment with distinct flora and wildlife. Explore the reserve's hiking paths to explore cactus, limestone formations, and the possibility to view diverse bird species. The Ballena Trail and Fort Capron Trail are popular alternatives for hikers.

Camuy River Cave Park: Underground Adventure: Embark on an underground journey at Camuy River Cave Park. Guided excursions lead you deep into the limestone caverns, where you'll cross rugged terrain, observe spectacular stalactites and stalagmites, and hear the relaxing sounds of the subterranean river. It's a unique and bizarre experience.

Culebra and Vieques: Island Exploration: Both Culebra and Vieques, situated close off the east coast of Puerto Rico, provide tremendous options for outdoor activity. Explore gorgeous beaches, trek along coastal paths, and snorkel in crystal-clear seas. In Culebra, trek to the summit of Mount Resaca for panoramic vistas, while in Vieques, take a stroll through the Vieques National Wildlife Refuge.

subterranean river via guided excursions. The unique geological formations and the underground realm make this park a fascinating excursion.

Reserva Natural de Humacao: Birdwatching Paradise

The Reserva Natural de Humacao on the east coast of Puerto Rico is a paradise for birdwatchers and environment enthusiasts. Explore the wetlands and mangrove woods on designated walking pathways and boardwalks. You may view a broad range of bird species, including egrets, herons, and the elusive Puerto Rican parrot.

Waterfall Adventures: Puerto Rico features various waterfalls that are accessible through hiking paths. In addition to El Yunque's La Mina Falls, you may visit other spectacular waterfalls including Charco Azul, Gozalandia Falls, and Juan Diego Falls. Each provides a distinct natural scenery and a pleasant location to take a swim.

From the lush jungles to the rocky mountains and scenic coasts, Puerto Rico's outdoor experiences offer to a broad variety of interests and ability levels. Whether you're trekking through deep forests, discovering subterranean tunnels, or lounging on quiet beaches, Puerto Rico's natural splendor attracts explorers to explore and uncover its hidden secrets.

Water Sports and Recreation

With its magnificent coastline, warm Caribbean seas, and year-round nice weather, Puerto Rico is a water sports enthusiast's heaven. Whether you're an adrenaline seeker seeking thrills or searching for a more laid-back aquatic experience, the island provides a broad assortment of water-based activities. Here are some of the best water sports and entertainment activities to enjoy in Puerto Rico:

Surfing: Riding the Waves: Puerto Rico is recognized for its superb surf conditions, drawing surfers from across the globe. Popular surf places include Rincon on the west coast, Maria's Beach near Aguadilla, and La Pared in Luquillo. Whether you're a seasoned surfer or a novice, you'll find the right wave to ride.

Snorkeling: Exploring Marine Life: The crystal-clear seas around Puerto Rico are teaming with marine life and colorful coral reefs. Snorkeling is a terrific method to explore the underwater world. Snorkelers may visit sites like Culebra's Flamenco Beach,

Vieques' Mosquito Pier, and Tamarindo Beach in Culebra for outstanding snorkeling experiences.

Scuba Diving: Deep-Sea Adventures: For more immersive study of Puerto Rico's underwater treasures, scuba diving is a necessary. The island provides diving locations for all skill levels, from shallow reefs to difficult deep dives. Divers may discover colorful fish, sea turtles, and even shipwrecks, like the Antonio López wreck near Ponce.

Kayaking: Coastal and River Adventures: Kayaking is a flexible water sport in Puerto Rico. Paddle along the island's shoreline, discover the bioluminescent beaches of Vieques and Fajardo, or traverse the peaceful rivers and mangrove forests, such as the Guajataca River and the Rio Camuy Cave Park.

Stand-Up Paddleboarding (SUP): Balance and Serenity: Stand-up paddleboarding has gained popularity in Puerto Rico for its calm but demanding experience. Rent a paddleboard and sail along the calm waters of Condado Lagoon in San Juan or explore the quiet canals of the Piñones Mangrove Forest.

Sailing and Boating: Island Hopping: Explore Puerto Rico's coastline and adjacent islands by chartering a sailboat or motorboat. You may travel to sites like Vieques, Culebra, and Mona Island, each providing distinct experiences, from quiet beaches to pure natural beauty.

Wind and Kite Surfing: Harnessing the Breeze: Wind and kite surfing aficionados may take advantage of the trade winds that favor Puerto Rico. Locations like Cabo Rojo and Dorado provide superb conditions for these exhilarating sports.

Whether you're seeking adventure, leisure, or a mix of both, Puerto Rico's many water sports and recreational activities provide something for everyone. With its unique aquatic habitats and spectacular coastline panoramas, the island offers the ideal setting for unforgettable water-based adventures.

Horseback Riding and Eco-Tours

Exploring the natural beauty and different ecosystems of Puerto Rico is a gratifying experience, and one of the finest ways to accomplish so is by horseback riding and eco-tours. These activities give a unique perspective on the island's scenery, animals, and cultural legacy. Here's a glance at the horseback riding and eco-tour choices available in Puerto Rico:

Horseback Riding: Riding Through Paradise: Horseback riding is a tranquil and immersing way to experience Puerto Rico's countryside, beaches, and beautiful woods. Whether you're an experienced equestrian or a beginner, there are guided horseback riding experiences available to accommodate all levels of ability. Some popular sites for equestrian riding include:

El Yunque National Forest: Explore the jungle on horseback and explore gorgeous pathways that lead you through lush flora and to cascading waterfalls.

Rincón: Ride through the beaches and coastal paths of this laid-back surf town on the west coast, where you can enjoy stunning ocean views.

Camuy: Experience a horseback excursion through the gorgeous countryside, with pathways that bring you to the spectacular Arecibo Observatory.

Culebra and Vieques: These islands provide horseback riding tours through beautiful beaches and across stunning surroundings.

Eco-Tours: Immersion in Nature: Eco-tours in Puerto Rico establish a strong connection with the island's natural beauty and cultural legacy. These guided excursions are aimed to educate and inspire while boosting conservation initiatives. Some eco-tour alternatives include:

El Yunque Rainforest Tours: Explore the unique flora and animals of El Yunque National Forest while learning about its value as a protected natural area. Experience guided walks, waterfall tours, and birding trips.

Lares Cultural and environmental Tours: In the town of Lares, eco-tours mix cultural encounters with environmental discovery. Learn about the history of Lares and its importance in Puerto Rican culture while enjoying treks in the local mountains and rivers.

Arecibo Observatory: While principally recognized for its radio telescope, the Arecibo Observatory provides tours that teach tourists about space exploration, astronomy, and the facility's scientific accomplishments.

Eco-tours and horseback riding trips in Puerto Rico not only enable you to interact with nature but also give insight into the island's rich history and culture. Whether you're exploring the jungle, kayaking through bioluminescent bays, or biking along gorgeous trails, these activities give a greater appreciation for Puerto Rico's natural treasures and conservation efforts.

CHAPTER 6 FESTIVALS AND CELEBRATIONS

A Calendar of Puerto Rico's Colorful Festivals

Puerto Rico is a dynamic and culturally rich island that knows how to celebrate. Throughout the year, the island comes alive with a calendar full of vibrant festivals and events that display its distinct combination of customs, music, dance, and food. Here's a taste of the celebratory vibe that greets you in Puerto Rico:

January

Calle San Sebastián Festival (Fiestas de la Calle San Sebastián): Held in Old San Juan, this bustling four-day celebration honors the conclusion of the Christmas season with music, dancing, art exhibitions, food sellers, and a dynamic street party atmosphere.

February

Carnaval de Ponce: Ponce, also known as the "Carnival Capital of Puerto Rico," presents a huge carnival celebration with colorful parades, loud music, traditional masks, and stunning costumes.

March

Event de la China Dulce: In Las Marías, this event celebrates the town's delicious oranges with music, dancing, and lots of citrus delights.

April

Festival de las Flores: Aibonito, the "City of Flowers," organizes this floral festival when the town's gardens and plazas are covered with magnificent flowers, and parades include flower floats and traditional clothing.

May

Festival de la China: Las Marias celebrates its other renowned fruit, grapefruits, with a festival that includes music, dancing, and, of course, grapefruit-themed meals and beverages.

June

Noche de San Juan: On the night of June 23rd, Puerto Ricans congregate on the beaches to celebrate the summer solstice with bonfires, music, and ceremonies.

Event del Güiro: Las Piedras presents this event devoted to the güiro, a traditional Puerto Rican percussion instrument. It features live music and contests.

July

Event Nacional de la Güira de Hatillo**: Hatillo's event commemorates the güira, a gourd-based instrument. Participants dress in bright clothes and perform music in a vibrant parade.

August

Semana del Jíbaro Puertorriqueño**: This week-long festival in San Sebastián highlights Puerto Rico's rural history, including festivities like traditional music, dancing, and folkloric performances.

September

Fiestas Patronales de la Virgen de los Remedios: Celebrated in Aguadilla, this festival features religious processions, music, dancing, and cultural displays.

October

Festival de la Guitarra: The town of Juana Díaz celebrates the guitar with concerts, recitals, and guitar-making workshops.

November

Fiestas de la Santa Cecilia: Celebrated in Ponce, this festival commemorates the patron saint of music with concerts, parades, and music-related festivities.

December

Fiesta de Santiago Apóstol: In Loíza, this festival commemorates St. James the Apostle with colorful parades, traditional Afro-Caribbean music and dance, and cultural displays.

Las Mañanitas a la Virgen de Guadalupe**: In the village of Vega Alta, this religious event features traditional music, dance, and a procession in honor of the Virgin of Guadalupe.

These are just a handful of the numerous events that Puerto Rico has to offer throughout the year. Whether you're enthusiastic about music and dance, interested in traditional crafts and food, or just wanting to immerse yourself in the vivid culture of the island, Puerto Rico's festivals give a colorful and unique experience. Be careful to verify the particular dates and locations of these activities before arranging your vacation to the island!

Joining in the Celebrations: Tips for Tourists

If you're planning a vacation to Puerto Rico and want to immerse yourself in the island's colorful festivals and cultural festivities, there are some recommendations and considerations to guarantee you have a good and respectful experience. Here are some useful recommendations for travelers seeking to partake in the festivities:

Before your journey, investigate the festival or event you intend to attend. Learn about its importance, history, and the program of events. Understanding the backdrop of the event will boost your enjoyment of the experience.

Many festivities in Puerto Rico incorporate colorful costumes, traditional garb, or special dress rules. Check whether there are any wardrobe guidelines or limits for participants, and consider attending by wearing acceptable clothes. This not only shows respect for the culture but also helps you to blend in and thoroughly enjoy the celebrations.

While many Puerto Ricans speak English, having some basic Spanish words at your disposal may go a long way in communicating with locals and demonstrating respect for their language. Simple pleasantries like "Hola" (hello) and "Gracias" (thank you) are welcomed.

Each event may have its unique customs and traditions. Be cognizant of these rituals and show respect by engaging in them when appropriate. For example, if there's a traditional dance or ceremony, watch and follow the lead of locals.

Politeness and decent manners are generally praised. Say "por favor" (please) and "gracias" (thank you) while engaging with natives, and always be respectful. Wait your turn in lines, avoid pushing or shoving, and be respectful of personal space.

Puerto Rico's celebrations frequently contain a broad choice of tasty native dishes and drinks. Be daring and sample native cuisine like mofongo, tostones, or empanadillas from street sellers. It's a wonderful approach to immerse oneself in the local culinary culture.

Some events may have prohibitions on photography or filming, especially during religious or holy activities. Always ask for permission before taking images of persons, and obey any stated restrictions about cameras and recording equipment.

Festivals may be raucous, and schedules may not always run on time. Embrace the laid-back island vibe, and be patient if things don't go precisely as planned. Sometimes, the unexpected moments make for the most unforgettable experiences.

By following these suggestions and showing respect for the local culture and customs, you'll not only have a more enriching and delightful festival experience in Puerto Rico but also build great relationships with the island's hospitable population. Joining in the festivities is a fantastic opportunity to connect with the heart and soul of this gorgeous Caribbean Island.

CHAPTER 7 PRACTICAL TRAVEL INFORMATION

Transportation and Getting Around

Navigating Puerto Rico is reasonably straightforward, with a range of transportation alternatives accessible for guests. From major cities to rural regions of the island, you may experience Puerto Rico's unique landscapes, culture, and attractions. Here's a guide on transportation and getting about in Puerto Rico:

Renting a Car: Vehicle Rentals: Renting a vehicle is a popular alternative for those who want the flexibility to explore the island at their own speed. important automobile rental businesses have offices at both airports and in important cities including San Juan, Ponce, and Aguadilla.

Driving standards: Puerto Rico follows U.S. driving standards, with driving on the right side of the road. Road signs are in English and Spanish. Be aware that transportation might be heavy in large cities, so plan appropriately.

Gasoline: Gasoline prices in Puerto Rico are comparable to those on the U.S. mainland. Gas stations are widespread, particularly in metropolitan areas.

Public Transportation

Buses: Public buses, known as "guaguas" or "públicos," serve many portions of the island, however the service might be restricted in rural locations. San Juan and Ponce have more extensive bus networks.

Taxis: Taxis are frequently accessible in cities and tourist locations. Make sure the taxi has a valid license and agree on the fee before commencing your journey. Taxis in big cities typically feature meters.

Ridesharing: Services like Uber and Lyft operate in Puerto Rico, particularly in San Juan and other large cities.

Ferries and Boats

Ferries: Puerto Rico has a network of ferries that link the main island with smaller islands like Vieques and Culebra. Ferry timetables might change, so it's a good idea to check in advance.

Boat Tours: Various boat tours are offered for enjoying the coastline splendor of Puerto Rico, including snorkeling expeditions, sunset cruises, and excursions to bioluminescent bays.

Air Travel

International Airports: The two major international airports in Puerto Rico are Luis Muñoz Marín International Airport (SJU) in San Juan and Rafael Hernández Airport (BQN) in Aguadilla. Both airports provide various local and international flights.

Regional Airports: The island has many smaller regional airports, making it easier to visit various sections of Puerto Rico. These include Ponce Airport (PSE), Mayagüez Airport (MAZ), and others.

Bicycle Rentals: Some neighborhoods, including Old San Juan, are bike-friendly and provide bike rentals. However, riding may be tough owing to traffic in metropolitan areas, so it's better ideal for leisurely trips in parks or along seaside walks.

Getting around Puerto Rico is an adventure in itself, with various landscapes, picturesque roads, and cultural experiences waiting to be found. Whether you prefer to hire a vehicle, depend on public transit, or explore on foot, the island's transportation choices make it accessible and easy to experience its beauty and attractions.

Accommodation Options: From Luxury Resorts to Cozy Inns

Puerto Rico provides a broad choice of lodging alternatives to meet every traveler's interest and budget. Whether you're seeking opulent resorts, modest inns, or somewhere in between, the island gives a range of alternatives for a pleasant and enjoyable stay. Here's a guide to the numerous hotel alternatives in Puerto Rico:

Luxury Resorts and Hotels: Puerto Rico features multiple world-class luxury resorts and hotels that provide top-notch facilities and breathtaking seaside surroundings. These high-end properties frequently have private beaches, golf courses, spas, great restaurants, and superb service. Some of the most notable luxury resorts include:

Dorado Beach, a Ritz-Carlton Reserve: Located on the northern shore, this resort provides unsurpassed luxury with beachfront villas, a famous golf course, and the hallmark Ritz-Carlton service.

The St. Regis Bahia Beach Resort: Nestled in a natural reserve in Rio Grande, this resort blends luxury with ecological protection. Guests may enjoy beautiful beaches and a Robert Trent Jones Jr. golf course.

Condado Vanderbilt Hotel: Situated in the center of San Juan's busy Condado area, this historic hotel provides magnificent accommodations, superb restaurants, and seaside views.

Boutique Hotels: For a more private and unique experience, try staying in a boutique hotel. These smaller resorts frequently offer customized service and unusual architectural aspects. Some popular boutique hotels include:

O:LV Fifty Five Hotel: Located in Condado, this boutique hotel provides contemporary décor, rooftop pool lounges, and individual service.

CasaBlanca Hotel: Situated in Old San Juan, this beautiful boutique hotel mixes colonial architecture with modern elegance and is within walking distance of historic places.

Vacation Rentals and Villas: Vacation rentals and villas are great for those who seek a home-away-from-home experience. You may discover a broad selection of alternatives, from beachfront condominiums to quiet villas in the highlands. Websites like Airbnb and VRBO give several possibilities around the island.

Cozy Inns & Bed and Breakfasts: For a more intimate and genuine stay, try renting a room at a quaint inn or bed & breakfast. These beautiful hotels frequently offer a warm and friendly environment. Some prominent inns include:

The Horned Dorset Primavera: Located in Rincon, this boutique hotel provides a romantic and serene location with magnificent accommodations and a famous restaurant.

Casa Sol Bed and Breakfast: Situated in the charming village of Rincon, this B&B offers a warm ambience, wonderful breakfast, and convenient access to beaches.

Budget-Friendly Hotels and Hostels: Travelers on a budget may discover inexpensive hotels and hostels across Puerto Rico. These lodgings offer necessary conveniences and are an ideal alternative for visitors wishing to tour the island inexpensively.

Santurce Hostel: Located in the Santurce area of San Juan, this hostel provides dormitory-style rooms and a shared kitchen for budget-conscious tourists.

Comfort Inn San Juan: Situated in the Condado neighborhood, this budget-friendly hotel offers pleasant accommodations and convenient access to the beach and attractions.

No matter your lodging choice, Puerto Rico provides a varied selection of solutions to suit to your requirements. Whether you're searching for a magnificent beachside vacation, a lovely boutique experience, or a budget-friendly stay, the island's lodgings are intended to make your visit memorable and comfortable.

Packing Tips and Essentials

Packing for a vacation to Puerto Rico involves careful consideration of the island's tropical temperature, different activities, and cultural experiences. To guarantee a pleasant and happy stay, here are some packing recommendations and important things to bring with you:

Lightweight apparel: Pack lightweight, breathable apparel such as shorts, tank tops, sundresses, and T-shirts. Choose moisture-wicking textiles to remain cool in the humid atmosphere.

Swimwear: Don't forget your swimwear, since you'll likely spend lots of time at the beach or at the pool.

Rain Gear: Puerto Rico sees intermittent rain showers, particularly in the jungle. A tiny umbrella or a wet jacket is helpful.

Comfortable Footwear: Bring comfortable walking shoes for touring, as well as sandals or flip-flops for beach activities.

Casual Evening Attire: Some premium restaurants and pubs may have dress rules, so it's a good idea to bring a couple somewhat dressier clothes.

Sunscreen: A high-SPF sunscreen is a necessary to protect your skin from the powerful Caribbean sun. Also, consider lip balm with SPF and after-sun lotion.

Sunglasses: Quality sunglasses with UV protection assist screen your eyes from the sun's brightness.

Broad-Brimmed Hat: A hat with a broad brim gives additional sun protection for your face and neck.

Beach Towel: Some lodgings may supply beach towels, but bringing a lightweight, quick-drying beach towel might be handy.

Snorkeling Gear: If you intend to snorkel, pack your mask, snorkel, and fins, but you can also rent these at most beach spots.

Reusable Water Bottle: Stay hydrated by carrying a reusable water bottle, and fill it up from filtered water sources.

Travel adaptor: Puerto Rico utilizes the same electrical outlets as the United States, so if you're coming from another country, you may require a U.S.-compatible adaptor.

Power Bank: Ensure your electronics remain charged with a portable power bank, particularly if you expect to be outside for lengthy durations.

Toiletries: While most hotels supply basic toiletries, carry travel-sized items of your preferred products to ensure you have what you need.

Prescription drugs: If you need prescription drugs, bring an extra quantity and copies of your prescriptions.

Basic First Aid Kit: Include products like sticky bandages, pain relievers, antacids, and other personal drugs you may require.

Passport and ID: Ensure your passport is valid for at least six months beyond your trip dates. Carry a copy of your passport and another form of government-issued ID.

Travel Insurance: Consider obtaining travel insurance that covers trip cancellations, medical emergencies, and misplaced baggage.

Printed Itinerary: Have a printed copy of your trip itinerary, hotel bookings, and any crucial contact information.

Reusable Shopping Bag: Puerto Rico has outlawed single-use plastic bags, so owning a reusable shopping bag is ecologically beneficial and handy.

Camera and Electronics: Don't forget your camera, smartphone, and any essential chargers and equipment to capture your moments.

Remember that Puerto Rico is a tropical vacation, so you'll likely spend a lot of time outside. Pack light, multipurpose attire, and don't forget to appreciate the local culture and food. With the appropriate basics, you'll be well-prepared to make the most of your vacation to this gorgeous Caribbean island.

Traveling Responsibly in Puerto Rico

Traveling ethically in Puerto Rico guarantees that you have a beneficial influence on the local environment, culture, and communities while enjoying your vacation to this lovely island. Here are some recommendations on how to be a safe visitor in Puerto Rico:

Leave No Trace: Practice the "Leave No Trace" principles by taking your waste with you, keeping on defined paths, and not disturbing animals or flora. Dispose of rubbish appropriately and recycle when feasible.

Conserve Water: Puerto Rico occasionally has water shortages, so use water wisely, particularly in drier locations. Report any leaks or water waste to authorities.

Support Sustainable Tourism: Choose tour operators and lodgings that have eco-friendly practices and support conservation initiatives.

Buy Local: Purchase souvenirs, crafts, and items manufactured by local craftsmen and buy at local markets to help the local economy.

Eat Local: Try local food and eat at locally-owned establishments. This not only helps local companies but also enables you to experience real Puerto Rican delicacies.

Stay at Locally-Owned Accommodations: Consider staying at locally-owned hotels, inns, and bed-and-breakfasts to directly assist the local community.

Learn About the Culture: Take the time to learn about Puerto Rican culture, history, and traditions. Respect local customs, festivals, and rituals.

Learn Basic Spanish: While many people in Puerto Rico understand English, learning a few basic Spanish phrases will help you communicate and show respect for the native language.

Ask Permission: Always ask for permission before taking photographs of individuals, particularly in rural or less touristic locations. Be attentive to cultural differences and privacy.

Eco-Tours: Choose eco-friendly tours and activities that concentrate on conservation, wildlife preservation, and responsible adventure tourism.

Bioluminescent Bays: When visiting bioluminescent bays like Mosquito Bay in Vieques or Laguna Grande in Fajardo, utilize tour operators who follow stringent protocols to safeguard these delicate ecosystems.

Reusable Bags: Puerto Rico has prohibited single-use plastic bags, so take a reusable shopping bag with you.

Refillable Water Bottle: Use a refillable water bottle and replenish it from filtered water sources to limit the use of single-use plastic bottles.

Say No to Straws: Politely refuse plastic straws when ordering beverages, or carry your reusable straw.

Don't Disturb animals: Avoid approaching or disturbing animals, particularly in natural settings like El Yunque Rainforest.

No Feeding: Do not feed wildlife, since it might upset their normal behavior and nutrition.

Switch Off Lights and Air Conditioning: When you leave your hotel room or vacation rental, switch off lights, air conditioning, and other energy-consuming gadgets.

Conserve Water: Be aware of water consumption, particularly in countries prone to drought. Report any leaks or water waste to housing personnel.

Respect Protected Areas: Adhere to laws and regulations in protected natural areas, including national parks and reserves.

Responsible Boating: If you're going boating or snorkeling, ensure you follow standards for marine conservation and avoid anchoring on coral reefs.

By exercising ethical travel behaviors, you may have a rewarding and delightful stay in Puerto Rico while contributing positively to the environment, culture, and communities. Being a considerate tourist helps preserve the island's natural beauty and legacy for future generations to enjoy.

CHAPTER 8 PLANNING YOUR TRIP

Creating Your Puerto Rico Itinerary

Puerto Rico provides a broad assortment of attractions, from ancient monuments and lush jungles to stunning beaches and dynamic towns. Planning your schedule in advance might help you make the most of your vacation to this wonderful island. Here's a step-by-step approach to planning your Puerto Rico itinerary:

Determine the Duration of Your Trip: Decide how many days you'll be spending in Puerto Rico. A week is a decent starting point, but you may customize your plan to meet a shorter or longer visit.

Identify Your Interests: Consider your hobbies and priorities. Are you seeking for a cultural experience, outdoor excursions, leisure on the beach, or a blend of everything? Understanding your preferences will determine your itinerary.

Choose Your Base: Select a few spots on the island where you'll stay for numerous nights. San Juan, the capital, is a popular option, but you could also like to visit other locations like Ponce, Rincon, or Vieques.

Plan Day-to-Day Activities: Break down your vacation into daily activities and experiences. Here's an example schedule for a one-week vacation to Puerto Rico:

Day 1-2: San Juan Explore Old San Juan's old streets, beautiful buildings, and historic forts (El Morro and San Cristobal).

- Visit institutions like the Museo de Arte de Puerto Rico or the Museo de las Américas.

- Enjoy real Puerto Rican food at neighborhood eateries.

- Experience the bustling nightlife of Condado or Isla Verde.

Day 3: El Yunque National Forest

- Take a day excursion to El Yunque Rainforest. - Hike the paths, explore waterfalls, and enjoy the beautiful environment.

- Learn about the rainforest's biodiversity and history at the visitor center.

Day 4: Luquillo and Fajardo

- Relax on Luquillo Beach, noted for its tranquil waves and attractive surroundings.

- Explore the bioluminescent bay in Fajardo with a guided kayak excursion (if visiting during the new moon).

Day 5-6: Vieques or Culebra

- Travel to Vieques or Culebra for a couple of days of tropical splendor.

- Relax on world-renowned beaches like Flamenco Beach or Sun Bay.

- Snorkel, swim, and discover the natural beauty of these little islands.

Day 7: Ponce or Rincon

- Depending on your tastes, select between Ponce (for art and culture) or Rincon (for surfing and beach vibes).

- Explore the Ponce Art Museum or Rincon's surf locations.

- Enjoy local food in the town of your choosing.

Be Flexible: While it's necessary to have a strategy, don't be scared to alter it as you go. Weather, surprising discoveries, and suggestions from locals may lead you to new experiences.

Identify the top sites or experiences that are must-see for you and ensure they're integrated into your agenda. For example, if you're a history lover, touring Old San Juan and its forts is vital.

Plan how you'll navigate about the island. If you're staying in San Juan, public transit or taxis are handy for city exploring. For day travels to areas like El Yunque or Fajardo, consider hiring a vehicle. If you're visiting Vieques or Culebra, plan your boat or flight in advance.

Include some leisure in your plan for relaxation and spontaneity. Puerto Rico's laid-back attitude promotes unhurried exploring and appreciating the present.

Check whether there are any events, festivals, or cultural festivities occurring during your stay. Attending local celebrations may offer a distinct and unforgettable experience to your vacation.

Be receptive to advice from locals and other visitors. Some of the finest experiences frequently come from unexpected discoveries and conversations.

Remember that Puerto Rico is a location that provides a varied variety of experiences, so personalize your itinerary to meet your interests and tastes. Whether you're touring the city, trekking in the jungle, or resting on the beach, Puerto Rico provides something for every tourist to enjoy.

Budgeting for Your Puerto Rico Vacation

Planning a budget for your trip to Puerto Rico is a critical step in ensuring you have a good holiday without overpaying. Puerto Rico provides a variety of possibilities for guests with varying budgets, from luxury resorts to budget-friendly hotels. Here are some recommendations for budgeting your Puerto Rico vacation:

Determine Your Total Budget: Start by determining an overall budget for your vacation. This should cover all significant costs such as airfare, lodgings, meals, activities, transportation, and souvenirs. Having a clear budget in mind can help you make educated selections during your vacation.

Book in Advance: Flight costs often change, so it's advised to book your tickets well in advance to receive the best rates.

Flexible Dates: Be flexible with your trip dates if feasible. Flights on weekdays or during the off-peak season tend to be cheaper.

Book Early: Like flights, lodgings may get more costly as the trip date approaches. Booking early may typically lead to better pricing.

Food and Dining: Local Eateries**: Opt for local eateries, food trucks, and casual restaurants to save money. Puerto Rican food is tasty and inexpensive.

Cook Your Meals: If you have access to a kitchen in your lodging, consider purchasing groceries and preparing part of your meals.

Transportation: Public Transport: Use public transit, such as buses or the Tren Urbano in San Juan, which is more budget-friendly than renting a vehicle.

Hiring a vehicle: If you want to go outside the city, consider hiring a vehicle for a few days. Car rentals are quite reasonable in Puerto Rico.

Keep track of your spending on your trip to verify you're remaining inside your budget. There are several budgeting applications and tools available to help you manage your expenditure.

Be Mindful of Tipping: Tipping is traditional in Puerto Rico, comparable to the United States. Budget for gratuities at restaurants, for tour guides, and other service providers.

Enjoy Affordable Adventures: Remember that there are many of low-cost or free activities and experiences in Puerto Rico, including hiking, beachcombing, and visiting diverse neighborhoods.

With careful budgeting and preparation, you may have a wonderful holiday in Puerto Rico without breaking the bank. Puerto Rico's natural beauty, rich history, and friendly friendliness make it a terrific destination for tourists on all budgets.

Safety Tips for Travelers

Puerto Rico is typically a secure location for tourists, but like any area, it's vital to keep cautious and take care to guarantee a safe and happy vacation. Here are some safety guidelines to keep in mind while vacationing in Puerto Rico:

Secure Your Belongings: Keep your stuff safe and avoid exhibiting costly goods like jewelry, gadgets, or big quantities of cash in public. Use a money belt or secret bag to hold vital papers and valuables.

Be Cautious in Crowded Areas: Be particularly vigilant in busy locations like tourist sites, public transit, and marketplaces, since these areas may be targets for pickpockets.

Use Reputable Accommodations: Choose well-reviewed lodgings with adequate security measures. Use hotel safes to secure your valuables, and lock your room while you're not present.

Avoid Walking Alone at Night: While many regions are secure during the day, it's recommended to avoid wandering alone in unknown or poorly lighted areas at night. Stick to well-lit streets and choose trusted transit choices like taxis or ridesharing services.

Stay Hydrated and Use Sun Protection: Puerto Rico's tropical climate may be hot and sunny. Stay hydrated by drinking lots of water, and wear sunscreen, sunglasses, and a wide-brimmed hat to protect yourself from the sun.

Know the Local Emergency Numbers: Familiarize yourself with the local emergency numbers in Puerto Rico. The emergency number for police is 911, and for medical situations, it's 787-343-2020.

Respect the Environment: Follow standards for conserving the environment, particularly while visiting natural places like El Yunque Rainforest or bioluminescent bays. Respect animals and respect to guidelines for conservation and safety.

Be Wary of Scams: Like any tourist location, Puerto Rico may contain scams or fraudulent activities. Be wary when contacted by strangers offering discounts or services that appear too good to be true.

culture will improve your experience and establish pleasant encounters with locals.

While Puerto Rico is typically a secure location, it's vital to be attentive and adopt common-sense measures to guarantee a trouble-free and pleasurable vacation. By following these safety guidelines, you may have a pleasant trip enjoying the island's natural beauty, colorful culture, and kind hospitality.

CONCLUSION

As we complete our thorough travel guide to Puerto Rico, we hope you are now well-prepared and motivated to go on your vacation to the "Island of Enchantment." Puerto Rico provides a unique tapestry of experiences, from exploring verdant jungles and stunning beaches to immersing yourself in its rich culture and relishing its exquisite food.

In Puerto Rico, you may gaze in amazement under tumbling waterfalls in El Yunque Rainforest, bask in the sun on magnificent Caribbean beaches, dance to the addictive rhythms of salsa, and relish the delicacies of its distinctive cuisine. You may also dig into the island's history, art, and culture at enthralling museums and lovely villages.

As you travel across Puerto Rico, remember to connect with the welcoming natives, who are always willing to share their culture and make you feel at home. Embrace the beauty of the natural environment, relish the gastronomic pleasures, and immerse yourself in the rich tapestry of Puerto Rican life.

Whether you're an explorer seeking exhilarating adventures or a visitor in quest of leisure and tranquillity, Puerto Rico has something to offer you. It's a location that blends the best of both worlds — natural marvels and lively culture.

As you construct your own Puerto Rico itinerary, take the time to discover hidden jewels, engage in local traditions, and cherish the moments that make your voyage truly yours. Puerto Rico welcomes you with open arms, asking you to experience its breathtaking beauty and culture, making memories that will last a lifetime.

So pack your luggage, immerse yourself in the charm of Puerto Rico, and let your journey begin. Whether you're a first-time tourist or returning to this Caribbean treasure, Puerto Rico offers an outstanding experience that will leave you with a profound appreciation for its beauty and a wish to return to this tropical paradise. ¡Bienvenidos a Puerto Rico! (Welcome to Puerto Rico!)

Useful Phrases in Spanish

When going to Spanish-speaking nations like Puerto Rico, understanding some basic Spanish phrases will enrich your trip and help you converse more successfully with natives. While many Puerto Ricans speak English, particularly in tourist regions, making an attempt to speak Spanish may be immensely appreciated. Here are some excellent Spanish phrases to get you started:

Greetings and Polite Expressions:

Hello - Hola

Good morning - Buenos días

Good afternoon/evening - Buenas tardes

Good night - Buenas noches

Please - Por favor

Thank you - Gracias

You're welcome - De nada

Excuse me / Sorry - Perdón / Disculpa (informal)

Yes - Sí

No – No

I don't understand - No entiendo

I don't speak much Spanish - No hablo mucho español

Can you assist me? - ¿Puede ayudarme?*

What is your name? - Cómo te llamas? (informal) / ¿Cómo se llama? (formal)

Basic Conversation

How are you? - ¿Cómo estás? (informal) /¿Cómo está usted? (formal)

I'm good, thank you- Estoy bien, gracias

What is this/that? - ¿Qué es esto/eso?

How much does this cost? - ¿Cuánto cuesta esto?

Where is..?- ¿Dónde está...?

I would like... - Me gustaría...

Do you have...? - Tiene...?

I need help - Necesito ayuda

I'm lost - Estoy perdido/a

Can you suggest a restaurant? - Puede recomendarme un restaurante?

Eating and Ordering Food

Menu - Menú

Water - Agua

Food - Comida

Breakfast - Desayuno

Lunch - Almuerzo

Dinner - Cena

Coffee - Café

Tea - Té

I would like a table for two - Quisiera una mesa para dos

The check, please - La cuenta, por favor

Delicious - Delicioso/a

I'm a vegetarian - Soy vegetariano/a

Shopping and Asking for Directions

Where is the nearest? - Dónde está el/la más cercano/a...?

How far is it? - A qué distancia está?

I'm seeking for... - Estoy buscando...

How can I travel to? - Cómo puedo llegar a...?

How much does it cost? - Cuánto cuesta?

Can I try this on? - Puedo probarme esto?

I'll take it - Me lo/la llevo

Emergencies

Help! - Ayuda!

I need a doctor - Necesito un médico

Call the police - Llame a la policía

I'm lost - Estoy perdido/a

I'm in trouble - Estoy en problemas

I've lost my passport - He perdido mi pasaporte

I'm not feeling well - No me siento bien

These simple Spanish phrases might be a great tool for your vacation to Puerto Rico. While many locals are multilingual, making an effort to speak their language may lead to more meaningful encounters and enrich your vacation experience. Puerto Ricans are often receptive of tourists who show an interest in their culture and language.

Made in the USA
Columbia, SC
08 October 2023